Russell Freedman

SHARKS

Holiday House / New York

Library of Congress Cataloging in Publication Data

Freedman, Russell.
  Sharks.

  Includes index.
  SUMMARY: A physical description of sharks and a
discussion of their methods of hunting, details of
birth, and their usefulness to humans.
  1. Sharks—Juvenile literature. [1. Sharks]
I. Title.
QL638.9.F74 1985   597'.31   85-42881
ISBN 0-8234-0582-6

A lemon shark taking a meal
© BOB GELBERG/PHOTO RESEARCHERS

This shark is doing what a shark does best. It's gulping down a
fish that was dangled in the water by a photographer. The shark
smelled the fish from a long way off and came racing over. It had
a tasty snack, and the photographer got a picture.

Every ocean contains sharks. They're most common in the warm waters of the Tropics. But they can be found in all the seas of the world, even near the poles.

Some sharks live in deep, dark waters at the bottom of the sea. Others stay near the surface, where they may bask in the sunlight or leap high into the air. A few sharks swim up rivers and live in freshwater lakes.

The smallest sharks are hardly bigger than minnows. A dwarf shark would fit comfortably in your hand. The biggest shark—the gigantic 50-foot whale shark—is longer than a Greyhound bus and weighs twice as much. Altogether, there are about 350 different kinds of fish that belong to the shark family. No one knows exactly how many kinds there are, because new sharks are being discovered all the time.

Sharks were swimming through ancient seas when dinosaurs walked on Earth. The sharks we see today look very much like their prehistoric ancestors. Sharks have survived for millions of years with little change because they are one of nature's most perfect designs.

Shark jumping in the Sea of Cortez, Mexico

Sharks are built for speed. Their streamlined bodies are designed to cut swiftly through the water. They're among the fastest of all fish. Blue sharks have been clocked at 43 miles an hour—faster than a racehorse.

A shark drives itself forward with powerful thrusts of its tail. Then it glides through the water as an airplane glides through air. The pair of fins behind its head—the pectoral (PECK-tur-uhl) or chest fins—look and act like an airplane's wings.

PECTORAL

FIN

Brown shark: fins like airplane wings

Brown sharks: built for speed
SEA WORLD PHOTO

If a shark stops moving, it will sink to the bottom. Other fish have a swim bladder, a kind of air-filled balloon, that keeps them afloat. They can stay at any depth without rising or sinking. A shark has no swim bladder. It must keep swimming or sink.

GILL SLITS

Tiger shark
COURTESY MIAMI SEAQUARIUM

A shark breathes with gills in the back of its mouth. As it swims, water flows into its mouth, over its gills, and out through its gill slits. The gills take oxygen from the water just as lungs take oxygen from the air.

Some sharks can lie quietly on the sea floor and breathe by moving their gills. But most sharks must swim with their mouths open in order to breathe. If they stop swimming, they will sink and drown.

A shark's skin looks sleek and smooth, but it's not. It is covered with hard sharp scales the size of grains of sand. Under a microscope, each scale looks like a pointed tooth, and that's just how it feels. If you rub a shark the wrong way, you can cut your hand.

A shark's skeleton is made of cartilage (KAR-tuh-lij) instead of bone. Your ears are made of cartilage, and so is the tip of your nose. A shark is all cartilage. It doesn't have a bone in its body.

Lemon shark
© RUSS KINNE/PHOTO RESEARCHERS

9

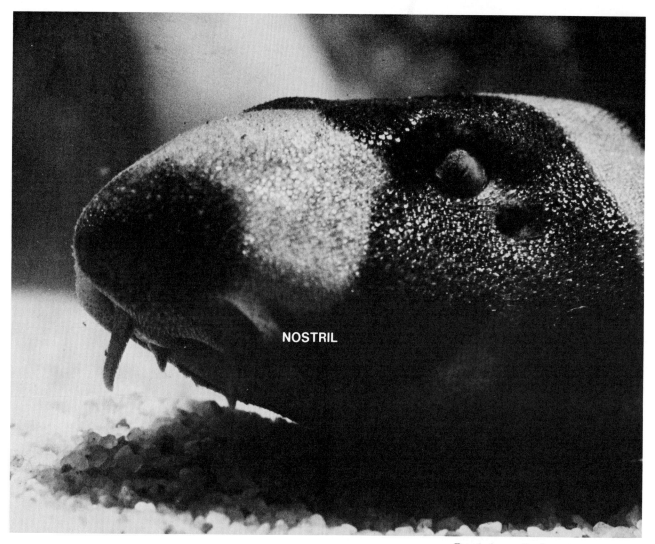

NOSTRIL

Banded cat shark
© TOM MCHUGH/PHOTO RESEARCHERS

When a shark hunts, it has a built-in search-and-destroy weapons system that helps it find and kill its prey.

It can smell blood from a quarter mile away. Once it picks up the scent, it swims toward the source like a guided missile. Its nostrils have nothing to do with breathing, since it breathes with its gills. The nostrils are only for smelling.

It has no ears, but it can "hear" sounds and movements in the water. Any sound or movement causes the water to vibrate. These vibrations are picked up by nerve endings on a shark's body and by special hearing organs in its head. A shark will swim toward the vibrations caused by a wounded or struggling fish.

As a shark gets close to its prey, it uses its big eyes. Most sharks see best in dim light. They hunt at dusk, at dawn, or in the middle of the night.

A shark also has a "sixth sense." Special pores on its face and snout can sense weak electric fields. Every living creature gives off a weak electric current when it is in the water. A shark can tell just where that current is coming from. A flounder may be buried in the sand, but it can't hide from a hungry shark. The shark can zero in on the faint current that gives the flounder away.

Jaws of a sand tiger shark
REX GARY SCHMIDT/U.S. FISH AND WILDLIFE SERVICE

A shark's jaws are lined with row after row of teeth that are sharp enough to shave with. Most sharks have four to six rows of teeth, but some have as many as twenty rows. In many sharks, the teeth tip forward when the jaws open and backward when they close.

Different kinds of sharks have differently shaped teeth. Some sharks use their teeth for cutting and sawing, some for grinding and crushing. By looking at a single tooth, an expert can tell what kind of shark it came from.

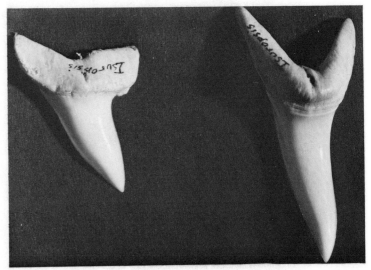

Two mako shark teeth

The teeth are always growing in a shark's mouth. They are not rooted firmly to the jaws, but are only loosely attached. As they get bigger, they move forward. The teeth in the front row do most of the work. As they wear down, they fall out and are replaced by teeth moving up from behind.

A young shark may get a new set of teeth every seven or eight days. As long as it lives, its teeth will keep growing, moving forward, wearing down, and falling out. In just one year, a tiger shark may grow, use and lose as many as 2,400 teeth.

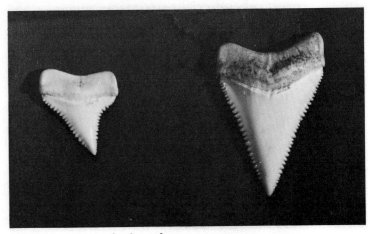

Two man-eater shark teeth

Lemon shark grabbing a fish . . .
COURTESY MIAMI SEAQUARIUM

. . . and pulling it under
COURTESY MIAMI SEAQUARIUM

Before a shark attacks, it may circle its prey for a long time. At first it circles slowly. Gradually it speeds up, swimming in smaller and smaller circles, getting closer and closer. Finally it moves in for the kill. At that point, nothing can stop a shark from attacking.

You can tell if a shark is going to attack by the way it moves in the water. A raised snout, an arched back, and chest fins pointed stiffly downward show that the shark means business.

Since its mouth is far back under its head, a shark usually attacks from below. It lifts its snout, opens its jaws, and lunges at its prey. If the victim is not too big, the shark will gulp it down whole.

Blood in the water can quickly cause a "feeding frenzy." Sharks will race to the scene from all directions. They will swarm around the bleeding prey, biting wildly, slashing at anything that gets in their way. If one shark is wounded and starts to bleed, the others will turn on it and rip it to pieces like any other prey.

Blacktip reef shark eating a mackerel
© TOM MCHUGH/PHOTO RESEARCHERS

Sharks usually eat other fish. But when fish are hard to find, they may take a bite out of anything they can catch. Some of the bigger sharks will attack and devour dolphins, seals, stingrays, sea turtles, sea gulls, and almost any kind of land animal that falls or is taken into the water. The remains of dogs, cats, cows, sheep, horses, and crocodiles have been found in the stomachs of captured sharks. Sharks have even been known to attack a crazed elephant that ran into the sea.

Big sharks eat smaller ones as a matter of course. A tiger shark caught in the Gulf of Mexico had a bull shark in its stomach. In the belly of the bull shark, scientists found a blacktip shark. And in the blacktip's belly, they found a dogfish shark.

Though sharks are scary, they're not always as dangerous as people think. Of the 350 different kinds of sharks, only thirty-nine kinds have been accused of attacking people. Most of those will attack only if they're threatened or annoyed. Fewer than a dozen of the bigger sharks can be called a real menace. They're the villains that have given all sharks a bad name.

According to one study, an average of twenty-eight serious shark attacks a year are reported from all over the world. Some attacks take place far out at sea, following plane crashes and ship sinkings. Others occur in shallow water close to shore, where people are wading, swimming, or diving. About two-thirds of the victims survive. Most of them never even see the shark that bites them.

Shark experts say that you can never tell what a shark is going to do. Scuba divers have moved freely among schools of sharks without being harmed. Usually the sharks ignore them or swim away. But divers have also been attacked, suddenly and without warning.

Great white shark
SEA WORLD PHOTO

The great white shark, also known as the man-eater, has probably attacked more people than any other shark. A typical great white, like the one shown here, is about 14 feet long. Its saw-edged teeth are thicker and longer than your thumb.

In Australia, spear fisherman Rodney Fox and shark photographer Valerie Taylor measured a white shark that swam alongside their boat. It was 24 feet long, making it the biggest great white on record.

Great white sharks are found in seas all over the world. They've been seen as far north as Newfoundland. Normally they eat animals like sea lions, sea otters, and elephant seals, along with their usual diet of fish. An adult great white can bite a seal in half. One great white, caught off the coast of Australia, had the remains of an entire horse in its stomach. Great white sharks have also been known to attack fishing boats and chew up ship propellers.

Despite its awful reputation as a man-eater, the great white shark doesn't seem to enjoy the taste of human flesh. After the first bite, most white sharks spit out their human prey. Some victims die from loss of blood, but most of them live to tell about it. They remember being lifted from the water by a huge fish, and then being dropped from its mouth.

Great white shark
COURTESY MIAMI SEAQUARIUM

Three tiger sharks

Tiger sharks have attacked almost as many people as great white sharks. And they're almost as big—up to 18 feet in length. If there's really a shark that will eat *anything*, it must be the tiger shark. Its diet ranges from crabs and snails to dolphin's tails. It also gulps down garbage that falls into the water. Unopened tin cans, lumps of coal, woolen overcoats, bicycle parts, and an entire chicken coop filled with feathers and bones have all been found in the stomachs of tiger sharks.

Bull sharks reach a length of 12 feet. They're dangerous because they hug the shore, prowling for food in shallow water where they may meet swimmers. They also swim up rivers. In the United States, they've been captured in the Mississippi River as far inland as Alton, Illinois—1,749 miles from the sea. They've also been found in the Amazon River in South America, the Ganges in India, the Zambezi in Africa, and in Lake Nicaragua in Central America.

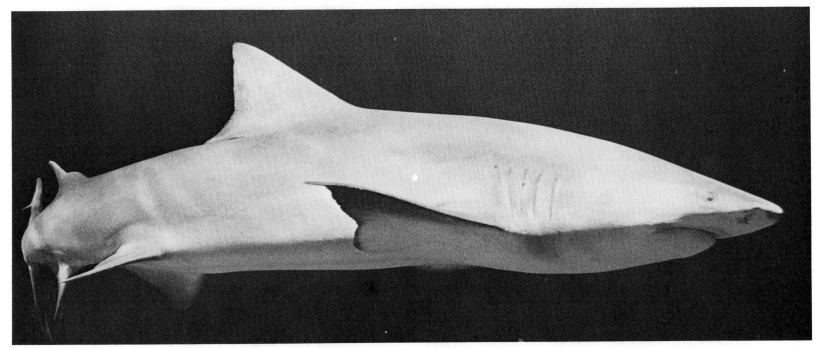

Bull shark
© 1985, SEA WORLD OF FLORIDA

Hammerhead shark
© RUSS KINNE/PHOTO RESEARCHERS

Another shark with a bad reputation for biting people is the strange looking hammerhead. Its head looks like a pair of stubby airplane wings. At the tip of each wing is an eye and a nostril.

The hammerhead's curious head probably helps it to hunt better. In a big hammerhead, the eyes may be 3 feet apart. Speckled across the entire head are tiny pores that sense electric fields. As the shark swims along, swinging its head from side to side, it samples a wide path of water. One thing is sure. Hammerheads are often the first sharks to arrive at the scene of bloodshed.

There are several kinds of hammerheads. The little bonnethead is only about 3 feet long, while the great hammerhead reaches 15 feet or more. Hammerheads live in all tropical seas, and they're found as far north as Nova Scotia.

Stingrays are their favorite food. They often search through shallow water for rays that lie buried in the sand. A hammerhead finds a buried stingray from the weak electric current the ray gives off. The shark noses the ray out of the sand and chases it around and around in a circle, biting at the ray's wings as it tries to escape. One captured hammerhead had nearly one hundred stingray spines in its head, jaws and mouth.

Two bonnethead sharks
© 1985, SEA WORLD OF FLORIDA

25

Approaching a harpooned whale shark

Size alone doesn't mean that a shark is dangerous. The two biggest sharks—the basking shark and the whale shark—are the only ones that are truly harmless.

All sharks are meat eaters, but basking and whale sharks live on the smallest creatures in the sea. They feed on plankton—tiny plants and animals that float on the sea's surface. These giant sharks swim slowly just beneath the surface, taking in huge mouthfuls of water. As the water streams through their gills, the plankton is trapped by sticky gill rakers that look like the bristles of a brush.

A typical basking shark is 25 or 30 feet long. The biggest ones are said to be 45 feet long. The largest whale sharks may reach lengths of 50 to 60 feet—almost as long as a bowling alley. They're the biggest fish in the sea.

Basking sharks live in cool northern seas, as far north as Newfoundland and the Gulf of Alaska. They seem to be basking in the sunlight as they swim slowly along. Whale sharks live in the Tropics. They're so slow moving, they've been caught by surprise and rammed by ships. And they're so gentle, swimmers have hitched rides by holding onto their fins.

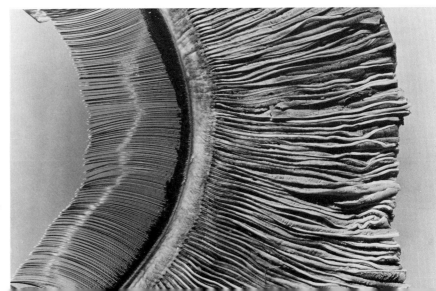

Gills of a basking shark. The bristle-like gill rakers on the left strain plankton from the water.
COURTESY AMERICAN MUSEUM OF NATURAL HISTORY

Banded cat shark
© TOM MCHUGH/PHOTO RESEARCHERS

Some of the most beautiful sharks are found among the cat sharks. Members of this family have colorful patterns of stripes, bars, and spots on their backs and sides. Most of them are small sharks, less than 3 feet long. They live in deep water throughout the Pacific, hunting for food along the sea floor. When a cat shark is threatened, it gulps water and swells up to three times its normal size.

The leopard shark is easy to recognize by the wide black spots and bands across its yellowish back and sides. It reaches a length of about 6 feet. Despite its name and savage appearance, the leopard shark is harmless. It's found along the Pacific Coast from Oregon to Mexico. Since it's one of the best tasting sharks, it's a favorite target of fishermen.

Leopard shark
© RUSS KINNE/PHOTO RESEARCHERS

Dogfish sharks are probably the most familiar of all sharks. They're common in both the Atlantic and Pacific. There are two kinds of dogfish sharks, belonging to two different families. While both kinds are harmless, fishermen regard them as real pests.

The spiny dogfish is usually less than 4 feet long. It has sharp spines growing out of the two fins on its back. It travels in big schools or groups, gobbling up smaller fish in its path and sometimes destroying fishermen's nets and gear.

Dogfish sharks
© ROBERT K. BRIGHAM/PHOTO RESEARCHERS

The smooth dogfish may be 5 feet long. It has no spines. It loves to eat shellfish, and it will raid fishermen's lobster beds whenever it has a chance.

College students get to know the spiny dogfish very well when they study zoology. That's the fish that they dissect (cut apart) as they study the organs of the body.

Smooth dogfish shark

Some baby sharks hatch from eggs. After the mother shark lays the egg, it becomes tough and leathery in the water. Attached to the egg case are long threads that cling to underwater rocks or plants. Inside is a developing baby shark. It gets its food from an egg yolk, attached in a sac to its belly.

A baby shark grows inside its egg for several months before it is ready to hatch. Empty egg cases, called "mermaid's purses," often wash up on beaches. Some may come from sharks, while many others come from their relatives, the skates.

Egg case of a swell shark
SEA WORLD PHOTO

Newly hatched swell shark
SEA WORLD PHOTO

Baby tiger shark
COURTESY MIAMI SEAQUARIUM

Most sharks give birth to living young instead of laying eggs. A tiger shark may have as many as eighty babies at one time. Each infant is about 2 feet long—longer than your arm.

Baby sharks are called "pups." They look like small copies of their parents. Nearly all baby sharks come into the world with their teeth in place and ready for action. It's a good thing, because they have to hunt for their own food from the beginning.

Sharks often travel with fish called shark suckers, or remoras (REM-ur-uhs). A remora has a flat disc on top of its head that acts like a suction cup. It uses its disc to attach itself to the nearest shark. Then it is carried about like a passenger clinging to a submarine.

Remoras don't just go along for the ride. When their shark attacks a fish and starts to feed, the remoras loosen their hold and swim over to dine on the scraps.

Sand tiger shark with remora clinging to its back

Sand tiger shark with three remoras clinging to its belly

The sharks don't seem to mind their passengers. In fact, they get something in return. Remoras pick tiny parasites from a shark's body. They help keep the shark clean as they hitchhike from one meal to the next. Remoras also attach themselves to whales, sea turtles, and the hulls of ships.

Small striped pilot fish travel with sharks, too. They swim close to a shark's head. They tag along for the same reason remoras do—to pick up food scraps.

It's true that some sharks will eat people, if they have a chance. It's also true that lots of people eat sharks.

Shark meat is a popular food in many parts of the world. When it's cooked right, it tastes like lobster. In England, the fish in fish 'n' chips is usually shark meat. In China, shark fin soup is considered a delicacy.

Almost every part of the shark from its jaws to its tail has a practical use. Shark teeth have been made into bracelets, necklaces, and earrings. Shark skin has been used by furniture makers as a fine sandpaper. When the scales are scraped off, the skin can be dried and tanned to produce one of the toughest and most expensive leathers in the world. Sharkskin leather is used to make shoes, handbags, billfolds, belts, and attaché cases.

Sharks may some day help cure human diseases like cancer. Cancer is common in many animals, but rare among sharks. Scientists believe that sharks may be protected from cancer by something in their cartilage or livers. If we can learn how sharks resist cancer, we may be able to prevent cancer in humans.

Boys with hammerhead shark
near Acapulco, Mexico
© TOM MCHUGH/PHOTO RESEARCHERS

Scientists also want to learn more about the lives and behavior of sharks. How smart are sharks? How long do they live? Where do they travel during the seasons of the year? Why do they attack people only at certain times? Can shark attacks be prevented?

Sharks are studied in aquariums and in the open sea. Scientists may watch the sharks from the safety of a steel cage that has been lowered into the water. Or they may put on diving gear and swim freely among the sharks.

A diver feeds a fish to a carpet shark at an aquarium in Sydney, Australia
AUSTRALIAN INFORMATION SERVICE

AUSTRALIAN INFORMATION SERVICE

Some scientists, photographers, and divers work with sharks day after day. They get to know each individual shark. Often they spend hours swimming among sharks, touching them, even feeding them, without being harmed. They may not come to love sharks, but they do learn to admire them for what they are.

People have always been fascinated by sharks. The more we learn about sharks and their place in nature, the less we need to fear them.

Index